MYSTERY DRIVER

MYSTERY DRIVER

The Story of Alice Johnson and the First Soap Box Derby

Elizabeth Tracy

illustrated by Anna Aronson

mit Kids Press

ALICE JOHNSON WAS BORN TO FLY.

On the ground, she was bookish and shy, but when she swooped through the clouds with Daddy, Alice felt as free as a bird. As they climbed the sky in their Swallow biplane, she believed she could do almost anything.

Now Alice and Daddy were grounded. The Great Depression had brought everything to a halt. There was barely enough money for food or clothes, let alone fun!

Then one day, something caught Alice's eye.

She wrinkled her nose. *Only for boys?*

For heaven's sake! Alice had flown through a tornado with Daddy when she was just three years old. The howling wind barely ruffled her feathers as she rode out the storm with her doll on her lap. Why couldn't she race a car too?

Alice grabbed a pencil and filled out the entry form, inscribing Daddy's name alongside her own.

Excitement for the derby spread like a prairie fire. Soon hundreds of challengers were signed up for the race— including one Mystery Driver.

To build her car, Alice knew she wouldn't need an engine or gas—just gravity and a clever design. But she'd never built anything before. Where would she even get supplies?

She watched the neighborhood boys cobble their contraptions together. They raided junkyards, basements, and garages, borrowing wheels from bicycles, baby buggies—even roller skates.

Some were real clunkers.

Others were a sight to behold!

Luckily, Daddy had a machine shop right next door—with spare parts and scrap metal aplenty. And he knew how to make a car go fast.

Ball bearings let the wheels spin smoothly.
Rubber tires absorb the bumps in brick pavement.
Sleek surfaces slice through the air.

But racing isn't just about speed. Like a pilot, a driver must master their controls.

Alice worked hard to build a rugged steering system and a set of friction brakes. Then came the crowning glory: an airplane's nose cone!

Every Sunday, Alice woke Daddy before dawn to practice. She learned to keep her eyes on the road, drive steady and straight, and press the brakes using just the right touch. Racing downhill was harder than it looked! But it sure felt good to sit in a cockpit again, and this time Alice was at the wheel.

Race day finally arrived!
Colorful bunting billowed like sheets in the breeze, and the smell of hot buttered popcorn filled the air. Vendors shouted over one another as the crowd pressed in. More than forty thousand people had turned out to watch.

Alice's stomach clenched tight. Her knees trembled. It would be easy to quit now. But Daddy was waiting on Burkhardt Hill. The whole family had flocked in to cheer Alice on.

Atop the hill, hundreds of boys paced in white racing helmets. Alice tugged her own helmet down and wove through the mob. She folded her legs and ducked inside her car, gripping the wheel until her knuckles turned white.

The challengers peered down the steep racecourse as they jostled into position at the starting line. Everyone drew a deep breath...

CRACK! The starter's pistol split the air.

The whole crowd roared.

Alice released the brakes and bumped downhill, gathering speed. Her heart hammered faster with each turn of her wheels. Her sleek design was working; Alice was in the lead!

Suddenly, her steering began to wobble. Her car veered toward the curb. Alice heard shouts and saw feet scrambling back onto the sidewalk. *I can't crash now!* she told herself.

Alice slammed on the brakes and yanked her steering wheel straight. Her car skidded and spun like she was caught in a hurricane. She was terrified, but she held the wheel steady—and regained control.

Now the boys were gaining momentum.

VROOM! One car shot past.

WHOOSH! Another streaked by like a blazing comet.

In a flash, Alice remembered: *Sleek surfaces slice through the air.* She leaned forward, hunching low in the cockpit. She was not going to let one more car pass!

Faster and faster she flew. A thrill coursed through her veins while the wind whipped around her and the sun beat down.

Seconds later, Alice barreled past the checkered flag and glided to a stop.

"WE HAVE OUR WINNERS!" boomed the announcer. Alice's car had finished third, but she felt like a grand champion.

When officials called her number at the awards ceremony, Alice strode forward, tore off her helmet, and shook out her curls.

Everyone gasped—a girl was in the race!

A murmur rippled through the crowd. Some folks grumbled, some chuckled, some dropped their jaws in disbelief. They all craned their necks for a closer look.

Then the first-place winner stepped up. He held out his prize bouquet and presented it to Alice. It was the largest bunch of roses she had ever seen.

The spectators burst into applause. Alice scanned the crowd and spotted Daddy, whose smile was beaming as bright as the sun—and her heart took flight.

What Made Alice's Car "Fly"?

THE PHYSICS OF SOAP BOX RACING

When Alice was little, household products like food and soap were shipped to stores in wooden crates. During difficult times, these sturdy boxes were often repurposed into useful items like tables, chairs, bookshelves—even race cars!

Not every car in Alice's race was made from a box, but they were all coasters—meaning they didn't have engines to make them go fast. Instead, winning drivers relied on physical forces to gain speed and to control their cars. Whether they realized it or not, all the competitors used ideas from physics when designing, building, and driving their cars.

A **force** is something that pushes or pulls on an object—like **gravity** and **friction**.

∞

GRAVITY

Gravity is what makes things fall down to earth. It's the main force that sets derby cars into motion and makes them go fast. Gravity pulled all the Soap Box Derby cars down steep Burkhardt Hill. But why did Alice's car go faster than most? There were other forces at work!

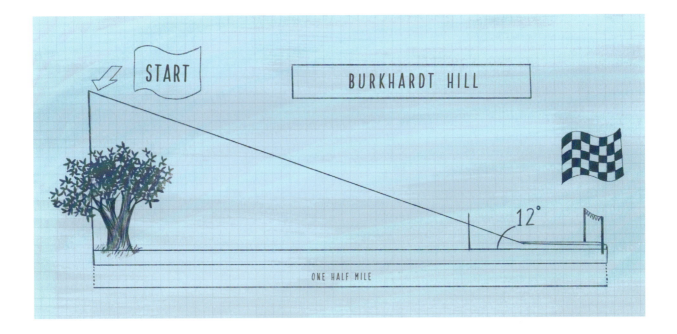

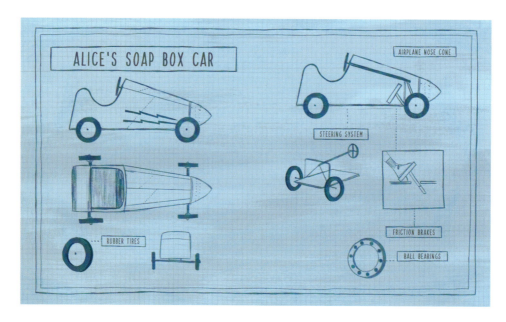

FRICTION

While gravity made the coasters go fast, friction slowed them down. The force of **friction** is the resistance of motion caused when one object rubs against another. Alice designed her racer to limit friction. She used ball bearings to minimize contact between the axles and the spinning wheels. She added a nose cone to "slice through the air" and reduce **drag**, which is friction from wind or air resistance. Special tires decreased surface friction from the rough brick road.

Alice's tires and brakes also *increased* friction—but in a good way! Quality tires helped keep her car on the road and heading in the right direction (instead of skidding or taking off), and friction brakes allowed her to slow down and stop once the race was over.

DRIVING SKILLS

In addition to constructing a well-built car, Alice understood that practice was key. Steering straight kept her route down the racecourse short and fast. Steady driving also diminished friction caused by swerving wheels and tires. Knowing when and how to apply the brakes kept Alice from crashing or veering off course. And in the final stretch of the race, she leaned forward in the cockpit to reduce wind resistance. Most of all, Alice understood the importance of working hard, driving safely, and being a good sport.

Alice and her father flew and drove together often, so they might have discussed Isaac Newton's **first law of motion**: An object at rest will stay at rest, and an object in motion will stay in motion—and keep moving in the same direction and speed unless forces act upon it.

Without the force of gravity, Alice and the other racers would never have made it down Burkhardt Hill. And without the force of friction, once their cars started rolling, they would never have stopped!

Selected Bibliography

Beans, Tawney. "Not Just a 'Boys' Race': Soap Box Derby Celebrates 50th Anniversary of Girls Racing." *Akron (OH) Beacon Journal*, July 24, 2021. https://www.beaconjournal.com/story/news/2021/07/24/girls-racing-soap-box-derby-mark-50th-anniversary-1971/7980389002/.

"40,000 Persons Witness First News Soap Box Races: Daring Youths Drive Cars at Record Speeds." *Dayton (OH) Daily News*, August 20, 1933.

Gale, Paul. "Physics Involved in Soap Box Derby Racing." Summary courtesy of the Marietta (GA) Soap Box Derby and Paul Gale. Mid-Missouri Soap Box Derby, September 4, 2008. http://www.midmosbd.org/sbd_physics.pdf.

Gambino, Megan. "The History of Soap Box Derby: For Nearly 80 Years, Kids Have Steered Their Gravity-Powered Racers Toward a Coveted National Championship." *Smithsonian Magazine*, June 30, 2011. https://www.smithsonianmag.com/history/the-history-of-soap-box-derby-25139930/.

"Mystery Driver in Soap Box Race." *Dayton (OH) Daily News*, August 2, 1933.

"Parade Opens Soap Box Race: 300 Youths in First Annual Youths' Event." *Dayton (OH) Daily News*, August 19, 1933.

Powell, Lisa. "Soap Box Derby: This World-Famous Event Was First Held in Dayton." *Dayton (OH) Daily News*, August 19, 2021. https://www.daytondailynews.com/news/first-soap-box-derby-featured-the-sublime-the-ridiculous/HE8owxaIKdpb8leA5nVI7N/.

Roberts, Bill. "Dares to Be Different: Joins First Soap Box Derby Race." *Marin (CA) Independent Journal*, July 30, 1973.

For Further Reading

Ferrie, Chris. *Let's Get Moving! Speeding into the Science of Motion with Newtonian Physics*. Naperville, IL: Sourcebooks eXplore, 2020.

Sohn, Emily. *A Crash Course in Forces and Motion with Max Axiom, Super Scientist*. Illustrated by Steve Erwin and Charles Barnett. North Mankato, MN: Capstone, 2016.

Swanson, Jennifer. *Explore Forces and Motion! With 25 Great Projects*. Illustrated by Bryan Stone. Norwich, VT: Nomad Press, 2016.

Author's Note

A FEW YEARS BACK, I was listening to a radio interview with a Soap Box Derby representative. He recounted the origins of the race, in 1933, when a group of Ohio boys coasting downhill in hand-crafted cars captured the attention of *Dayton Daily News* photographer Myron Scott. Scott asked the paper to sponsor a race for Dayton-area boys, and hundreds signed up! One girl named Alice Johnson also enlisted (although girls weren't welcome until 1971). Nobody knew she was there until she took off her helmet to receive her prize. I sat up straight. *Who was this brave girl who took the first derby by storm? How did she sneak in? And why weren't girls allowed?!*

I was on a quest to learn the story of this mysterious driver, so I made a beeline to my local public library, the Ohio Genealogical Society, and the *Dayton Daily News* archives. The title of this book, *Mystery Driver*, comes from a headline that appeared in the *Daily News* prior to the first race. I wasn't certain the headline referred to Alice, but the moniker sure fit! My real breakthrough came when I reached out to Alice's family. They answered my questions, trusted me with their archives and memories, and even shared a personal account Alice wrote about her racing experience. I've used much of that chronicle to tell her story.

Alice Johnson was the only girl—among 361 boys—to compete in the first Soap Box Derby. Like her father, pioneer aviator Edward Albert "Al" Johnson, Alice must have had an extra store of courage. She grew up on the grounds of her father's airfield, and the two flew together often in open cockpit planes. People around town dubbed Alice "the World's Youngest Aviatrix."

At the airfield, Alice met the likes of Orville Wright and Amelia Earhart. She was inspired by her father, and these other brave aviators, to compete in the race. Alice was ahead of her time when she signed up for the derby, built a winning car, and placed third in her class. (Some sources say Alice placed second; however, Alice's own written recollections, and newspaper accounts from 1933, indicate she placed third.)

The next year, in 1934, the Soap Box Derby became a national event, drawing even more drivers and spectators. Alice raced once more, challenging over four hundred boys and inspiring one other girl, Evelyn Beddies, to join the fun. A Black boy named George "Abe" Welch also took part, defying segregationist norms of the time. Alice placed third again—earning a football for her prize.

In 1935, the derby moved to Akron, Ohio. Previously, the race had been promoted as an event for boys only, but in 1935 girls were effectively prohibited. Alice and Evelyn were the last girls to compete until 1971, when a handful of racers and their mothers fought to allow girls.

With determination fueled by her racing experience, Alice forged ahead. She won prizes at school and graduated as valedictorian of her high school class. After college, Alice enlisted as an officer with the Navy WAVES (Women Accepted for Volunteer Emergency Service) and served during World War II.

Later, she married and moved to California to raise a family. Her cousin Jane, who had supported Alice during the first soap box race, also lived in California. Jane had married a mischievous young man named Randy Custer—the gallant grand champion who presented Alice with his flowers at the first derby!

In her own quiet way, Alice fought for inclusivity and set an example for others. Now women routinely serve in the military, and girls outnumber boys in some soap box races. Girls have set many important derby records and have paved the way for *all* kids, including nonbinary racers and kids with disabilities, to participate.

For all the hidden heroes of this book—
including Alice's family, my family, and amazing librarians everywhere
ET

For Jude, Hazel, and Amos
AA

∽

Text copyright © 2025 by Elizabeth Tracy
Illustrations copyright © 2025 by Anna Aronson

All rights reserved. No part of this book may be reproduced, transmitted, or stored in
an information retrieval system in any form or by any means, graphic, electronic, or mechanical, including
photocopying, taping, and recording, without prior written permission from the publisher.

The MIT Press, the ☰mit Kids Press colophon, and MIT Kids Press are trademarks of The MIT Press,
a department of the Massachusetts Institute of Technology, and used under license from The MIT Press.
The colophon and MIT Kids Press are registered in the US Patent and Trademark Office.

First edition 2025

Library of Congress Catalog Card Number pending
ISBN 978-1-5362-3157-1

25 26 27 28 29 30 CCP 10 9 8 7 6 5 4 3 2 1

Printed in Shenzhen, Guangdong, China

This book was typeset in Libre Clarendon.
The illustrations were created digitally.

MIT Kids Press
an imprint of Candlewick Press
99 Dover Street
Somerville, Massachusetts 02144

mitkidspress.com
candlewick.com

EU Authorized Representative: HackettFlynn Ltd., 36 Cloch Choirneal, Balrothery,
Co. Dublin, K32 C942, Ireland. EU@walkerpublishinggroup.com

Elizabeth Tracy loves real-life inspiring stories, especially when they feature empowered women and girls. She hasn't raced in a gravity-powered car—yet. But it's never too late to try! As well as being a children's writer, she's been a businesswoman, professor, and proud mother of two mighty girls. She lives with her physics-defying husband in New York State, where they divide their time between Manhattan and the scenic Hudson Valley.

Anna Aronson lives in Wisconsin, America's dairy land. In her art, she loves to capture scenes from everyday life, both present and historical. She revels in the challenge of conveying the richness of human experiences in visually captivating ways. In addition to her work, Anna Aronson lives on a small hobby farm with her family and an ever-growing menagerie of animals.